APR   2015

A Kid's Guide to
THE MIDDLE EAST

Understanding
IRAQ
Today

IRAQ

Will Blesch

Mitchell Lane
PUBLISHERS
P.O. Box 196
Hockessin, Delaware 19707

A Kid's Guide to
THE MIDDLE EAST

Zakhu
Dahuk
Dahuk
'Aqrah   Rayat
Sinjar Al Mawsil   Arbil
                  Qal'at Dizah
                  Irbil
Ninawa   As Sulaymaniyah
        At Ta'min   Kirkuk
                    As Sulaymaniyah
Salahad Din   Ba'iji
             Tikrit
Al Qa'im   Khanaqin
         Samarra'   Diyala
Al Hadithah
         Ar Ramadi   Ba'qubah
Al Anbar   Mandali
                   Baghdad
Ar Rutbah Iraq
                   Wasit
         Karbala'   Al Kut
              Karbala' Al Hayy   Maysan
Nukhayb   An Najaf Ad Diwaniyah
                   Al Qadisiyah   Al 'Amarah
         An Najaf   As Samawah   Dhi Qar
                        An Nasiriyah
                            Al Basrah
              As Salman
              Al Muthanna   Al Basrah
         Makhfar al Busayyah   Umm

TURKEY

SYRIA
LEBANON
           IRAQ
PALESTINE
ISRAEL   IRAN   AFGHANISTAN
         JORDAN

         SAUDI
         ARABIA

Mitchell Lane

PUBLISHERS

Copyright © 2015 by Mitchell Lane Publishers, Inc. All rights reserved. No part of this book may be reproduced without written permission from the publisher. Printed and bound in the United States of America.

Printing   1   2   3   4   5   6   7   8   9

Library of Congress Cataloging-in-Publication Data
Blesch, Will.
 Understanding Iraq today / By Will Blesch.
    pages cm. — (A kid's guide to the Middle East)
 Includes bibliographical references and index.
 ISBN 978-1-61228-648-8 (library bound)
 1. Iraq—Juvenile literature. I. Title.
 DS70.62.B54 2014
 956.7044'3—dc23
                                                            2014021280
eBook ISBN: 9781612286716

PUBLISHER'S NOTE: The narrative used in portions of this book is an aid to comprehension. This narrative is based on the author's extensive research as to what actually occurs in a child's life in Iraq. It is subject to interpretation and might not be indicative of every child's life in Iraq. It is representative of some children and is based on research the author believes to be accurate. Documentation of such research is contained on pp. 60–61.

The Internet sites referenced herein were active as of the publication date. Due to the fleeting nature of some web sites, we cannot guarantee they will all be active when you are reading this book.

To reflect current usage, we have chosen to use the secular era designations BCE ("before the common era") and CE ("of the common era") instead of the traditional designations BC ("before Christ") and AD (*anno Domini,* "in the year of the Lord").

PBP

CONTENTS

BOLD words in text can be found in the glossary

Introduction

Iraq is a country in the Middle East and is nicknamed "The Cradle of Civilization." This is because many thousands of years ago, some of the world's first major cultures became empires and rose to great power there. Some of these empires included ancient Sumeria and Babylon. While these massive kingdoms were ascending, many other people lived in less advanced cultures elsewhere.

In today's world, Iraq is a country that borders the Persian Gulf. Its neighbors include the Middle Eastern countries Turkey, Syria, Iran, Jordan, Kuwait, and Saudi Arabia. The majority of people are **Arabs**, although there are also **Kurds**, **Turkomans**, **Assyrians**, and **Armenians**. The largest religion is Islam, with a very small minority of **Christians** and others.

The country has two major landmarks. These are the Tigris and Euphrates rivers. That's why its other nickname is "The Land of Two Rivers." Not many years ago, Iraq was ruled by the dictator, Saddam Hussein, but today the country is run by a parliamentary democracy. This is similar to the government of Great Britain. In Iraq, the head of the government is the Prime Minister.[1]

Kufa Mosque is one of the oldest mosques in Islamic Iraq. It is located in the city of Kufa, in the province of Najaf, Iraq.

In today's Iraq, there are things that are both good and bad. For example, Iraq is an oil rich country. It sends more oil to other countries than any other nation in the Middle East except Saudi Arabia. The truth is, the nation is rich when it comes to many natural resources. These resources produce a lot of money for Iraq. This doesn't mean that its people are wealthy, though. Many regular people believe that officials in the Iraqi government keep the money from oil for themselves and are angry about it. A lot of people are unemployed, and government services and healthcare are very poor. Things like clean drinking water, usable bathrooms and toilets, things most Americans take for granted, are luxuries to the majority of Iraqis today. These are negative things that must be improved.

In today's world, Iraq is an unstable place. Sadly, it is considered to be one of the most dangerous countries in the world today. Some type of violence occurs on a daily basis. Some countries around Iraq wait to see if they can benefit from this violence, while others hope to see Iraq become safe and peaceful. The entire world watches and waits to see what will happen in the coming years.

Around 8:30 in the morning, most kids catch the bus to school. These girls live close enough that they can walk.

CHAPTER 1
A Kid's Life in Iraq

Fatima Awad grew up in Iraq before her family moved to America to try and make a better life. She still remembers what life in Iraq was like for kids. "We got up around 7:00 in the morning, had breakfast, and then went straight to school," she recalls. Kids like Fatima often have a small cake and hot tea, or maybe eggs with cheese and pita bread for breakfast. Afterwards, around 8:30 in the morning, they have to catch the school bus. Some kids live close enough they can walk. At school, things are formal. Children are not allowed to call teachers by their first names. "I had to call my teacher Mr. Hamdani," Fatima said.[1]

At school, boys and girls attend class together. They learn many of the same subjects American kids do, like math, foreign languages, and history. However, there is no separation of church and state in Iraq. Public schools teach a mix of Islamic texts and other religious instruction. Another big difference is the fact that since 2003, teachers are not allowed to teach their students about the rule of Saddam Hussein. In like manner, they are also not allowed to teach their students about the American invasion of Iraq.[2]

There's a recess just like in American schools but when it's time for lunch they have to eat something prepared at home. Fatima noted that, "Most Iraqi schools don't have cafeterias." If kids misbehave, they are not sent to the principal's office. They don't get detention. Instead, they are prevented from participating in fun activities. By 3:30, school is done and most kids are at home.

Iraqi kids have to learn Arabic and a foreign language in school. These Iraqi Kurdish girls are studying Arabic.

After school, in the evenings, extended family may come over for a visit. Family is very important in Iraq. In fact, Fatima noted that unlike many American families, "Grandparents have a key role in the household." Grandparents usually live with their children and grandchildren for life! Because of this living arrangement, they are very close to the children. In the same way, kids usually live at home with their parents and grandparents until they get married. That might not happen until the kid is over thirty years old!

Family life is often structured around life events and religion, which impacts everyday life for almost everyone. "Religion is pretty big. Islam defined the way I dressed every day. It still does," Fatima said. "I also pray five times a day, every day." On Fridays, **Muslim** parents take their kids with them to the local

IN CASE YOU WERE WONDERING

What do Muslim men wear?
Some Muslim men wear a white (or brown or grey) one-piece cotton garment called the disdasha, and a head cover known as the ghutra. This is supported by a black ring, called the igal. However, in Iraq, many men wear western style clothing that is similar to clothes worn in other parts of the Western world.

mosque. "We wear modest, loose clothing. While there, we pray and worship."

Just like in America and Europe, kids in Iraq go shopping at malls, they play sports, and they listen to music. "I love shopping, but there are only a few malls to choose from." Soccer is the most popular sport in Iraq and lots of kids play it, although in Iraq they call soccer football. Basketball, kickboxing and wrestling are also popular sports, although these are played more as kids get older.

When it comes to music, kids go to concerts. The musical style though, is very different from others around the globe. It has a Middle Eastern sound, with lots of stringed instruments, drums, and woodwind instruments like the Moroccan oboe. "My favorite singer is Kathim Al-Saher. I love him. He's authentic, and he stayed true to his roots," Fatima said.

Kids also watch movies. Iraqi films are usually dramas, comedies, or documentaries, although not many films have been made since the fall of Saddam Hussein. There is also live theater and opera in Iraq, but many kids don't go to them.

IN CASE YOU WERE WONDERING

Do kids play games at home?
Yes. In fact, Mancala is one such game. It is believed to be the oldest board game that is played using colored marbles or beads. The object of the game is to place all of your marbles in the "scoring pit" and capture your opponent's marbles.

Just like in other parts of the world, kids in Iraq go shopping at malls. This Iraqi boy is having some fun at an arcade in the Zawra Park.

In the summer, parents often take their kids on vacations. Popular places to go include religious shrines, usually associated with the Prophet Muhammad. For example, Najaf is a city where thousands go to see the Shrine of Imam Ali. The shrine is a golden domed structure filled with very expensive objects, which are gifts made by kings and important people. Next to Imam Ali's shrine is the world's second largest cemetery. Several different prophets important to Islam are buried there, and today Muslims from all over the world feel that it is an honor to be buried there as well. Fatima said she had never been to any of these shrines, but that she "always heard about and wanted to see them."

IN CASE YOU WERE WONDERING

What do Muslim women wear?
Many Muslim women wear an abaya (ah-BAY-uh), which is a simple, long black dress with a headscarf called a hijab. Some Muslim women will add a face cover called a burkha.

GOING TO CONCERTS IN IRAQ

You probably like watching MTV. But, have you ever been to a live concert? If you have, then you know it can be an amazing experience. Going to a concert in Iraq can be risky and difficult though. You see, there are still concerts in Iraq, but many of the country's most famous musicians left during the rule of Saddam Hussein. Some who didn't flee the dictator's rule left after the American invasion of Iraq. All were fleeing violence of one kind or another.

Many places that used to hold concerts shut down. Kids want to go to concerts there, just like they do in other areas of the world, but even with some famous singers coming back to Iraq, the concerts are not always safe. In fact, unlike in America, where kids have no problem seeing artists like Justin Bieber, going to a concert in Iraq could be a life-risking event. Just to get in to the concert, people have to go through several check-points where guards search them for weapons. After being searched by guards, concert goers have to allow sniffer dogs to smell them . . . just to be sure they are not carrying a bomb of some kind.

Iraqis at a concert

Once inside the concert hall, there are many armed security guards. If one does attend a concert and gets past all the security, concert goers can then enjoy the live music of artists like Naseer Shamma. A legend among lovers of the region's traditional instruments, Shamma has played the lute-like oud since the age of eleven. Events like the one where Shamma played are trying to bring live, traditional music back to Iraq. Shamma said "I love to play at popular places, not so much like here with lots of security outside. I want my friends to come and young people. I prefer smaller venues, it is more intimate, the feeling is deeper." Naseer Shamma's saxophone player, Hamid al-Badri said, "I left Iraq ten years ago because **al Qaeda** tried to kill me because I am an artist. For them, musicians were **haram**. Now Iraq is different, this is beautiful. This is the first time for me to play here since I left."[3]

This is an ancient sculpture of a god, one of the Annunaki from Sumerian culture, on display in New York.

CHAPTER 2
History and Government

Iraq has one of the longest histories of any place on earth. Reaching far back into the mists of time, you'll discover the rise and fall of empires. The dawn of civilization in Mesopotamia saw the rise of the Uruk culture that built some of the world's first cities, and the **Sumerians** who built the world's first **ziggurat**, a type of pyramid with a flat top.[1] In addition to the Uruks and the Sumerians, other famous empires that rose in Iraq include ancient Babylon and Parthia. Early Iraq was also one of the birth places of the Bronze Age, a time period in human history when men began using copper, and began to form writing systems.[2]

Throughout Iraq's history, various cultures invaded the land, conquered, and then fell as other peoples invaded and, in turn, conquered them. In the 7th century CE, The Muslims conquered Iraq, and in 1500, the land passed into the hands of the Ottoman Turks. From that time until World War 1, the Turks controlled Iraq. When World War 1 ended, Iraq left the **Ottoman Empire's** control and became a part of the British Mandate. Iraq became an independent country in 1932, but what we know as Iraq today did not come about until 1945. The country went through several periods of unrest until 1979 when a military man named Saddam Hussein came to power. A terrible war between Iraq and the neighboring country of Iran soon followed. That war lasted from 1980–1988.

In 1990, Saddam Hussein ordered an invasion into another neighboring country. This time, Iraq was going against Kuwait. However, the world was against this invasion and the United

Nations (UN) led by a military force from the United States forced Saddam to pull his army back to Iraq. Afterwards, Kurds in the north and **Shia** Muslims from the south decided to fight against Saddam Hussein's government. Saddam brutally crushed their rebellion, killing thousands of his own people. Eventually, the world had had enough. Again the United States invaded Iraq. This time it was in March, 2003.

This was a scary time for families throughout Iraq. Fatima remembers those difficult times. "It was a very scary time. Our lives were threatened," she said. "The US Military was going around arresting everybody. They even arrested my uncle. But under Saddam it was worse."[3]

During the American invasion, Saddam Hussein fled but was eventually captured. He was executed by the new Iraqi government in December, 2006, for crimes against the Iraqi people. Iraqi Prime Minister Nouri al-Malaki became the recognized head of the Iraqi government during this time period.

Since then, Iraq has been ruled by a parliamentary democracy. After the new government was put into power, the Iraqi people were guaranteed basic rights that had been denied to them under Saddam Hussein's government. Even so, this was a time of great unrest. The UN reported that more than 100 people per day were being killed in violence. Fatima noted that, "There are lots of people who were unhappy with Iraq's new government. My parents didn't like it. But, they liked the dictatorship of Saddam even less. Eventually, they had the opportunity to move to the United States, so they took it. It was safer, and there was more freedom to make a better life."

Iraq's new government has an executive branch with one president. However, they have up to three vice presidents, whereas the US has only one. Moreover, the Iraqi government has a prime minister, three deputy prime ministers, and at least thirty different cabinet ministers![4] Iraq's legislative branch (the branch of government that makes laws) is different from that of the United States, too. In America, there are two houses. They consist of the House of Representatives and the Senate. In Iraq, there is only one house. This is called the Council of Representatives (COR). It has 275 members, and each one serves a term of four years.

Since Saddam Hussein fell, the Iraqi government has tried to rebuild ties with the international community. At least fifty-

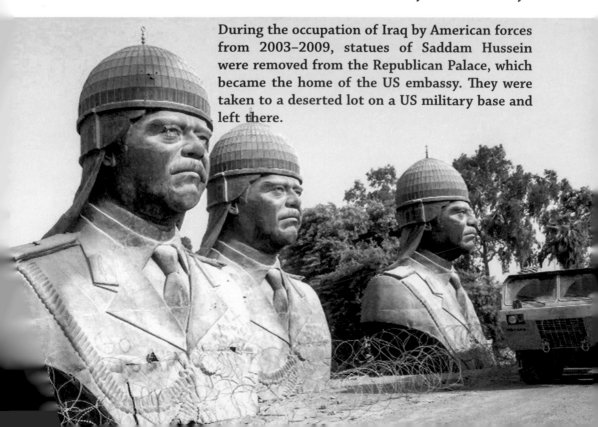

During the occupation of Iraq by American forces from 2003–2009, statues of Saddam Hussein were removed from the Republican Palace, which became the home of the US embassy. They were taken to a deserted lot on a US military base and left there.

four countries around the world have diplomatic relations with Iraq. The country is a member of the United Nations and is a full member of The Arab League in Cairo.

Even so, violence seems to continue throughout Iraq, despite the fact that it is no longer a dictatorship. The country is not safe for most kids. This quote from a BBC World News report states, "One Iraqi woman told BBC Arabic that children were still exposed to violence on a daily basis and there were no programmes designed to deal with the psychological problems this causes."[5] In fact, a lot of parents find their kids playing war, pretending to kill each other. One Iraqi man believes this is because they have no sense of hope. "Their lives have become meaningless," he said. "They don't know what they are doing. Most of them have become aggressive, even when they play."[6]

There are some who suggest that it is only a matter of time before the new government falls and the country descends once again into a terrible time of violence. "Violence has increased over the past two years and since December 2012, 692 children and young people have been killed and another 1,976 injured in violent attacks . . . With the growing political differences, violence and lack of security, as well as the regional tensions created by the Syria conflict, there is a general and an inevitable risk of total collapse of the state of Iraq."[7]

Where will the nation go from here? What kind of future will the kids of Iraq live in? Is there an Iraqi child that dreams of becoming a leader the people can believe in? Will Iraq's children grow into adults who will work together to bring peace back to this war torn country?

Only time will tell.

THE SUMERIANS:
LAND OF THE CIVILIZED KINGS

Did you know that ancient Iraq, the land of the Sumerians, was the home to mankind's earliest form of writing? It's true, and it's just one of the reasons ancient Sumer was called "The Land of the Civilized Kings." The type of writing they originally developed came in the form of pictures, which represented ideas. However, because the only material the Sumerians had to write on was clay, and writing on clay is hard, the Sumerians came up with a genius idea. They decided to turn the pictures into a series of wedge-shaped signs. These signs were then pressed into clay tablet with the help of an instrument called a **stylus**. The form of writing they came up with is known today as **cuneiform**. Reducing the writing system from pictures to wedge-shaped signs was a good idea. This is because, in the beginning, cuneiform had over 1,000 characters writers had to memorize![8] Eventually, they got that number down to only 600. Compare that to only twenty-six letters in the English alphabet!

"This great technological advance allowed news and ideas to be carried to distant places without having to rely on a messenger's memory. Like all inventions, writing emerged because there was a need for it."[9] The Sumerians needed to be able to keep records. But that's not the most interesting thing about it. Cuneiform is also the first system of writing to record religious thoughts and ideas. One of the world's first major stories, called "**The Epic of Gilgamesh**," was also recorded in cuneiform.

A cuneiform tablet containing "The Epic of Gilgamesh"

During a demonstration in Iraq's capital city, Baghdad, supporters of Iraqi Prime Minister Nuri al-Maliki carry his picture through the crowd.

CHAPTER 3
Current Issues

Serious issues face Iraq today. Although the country is no longer a dictatorship, violence occurs everywhere, even in cities with large security forces. Safety and bringing the divided country into a true state of togetherness is a main goal of the current government. But, this is a hard task. The Iraqi government is full of individuals who use the police, and even some army men, to frighten those who disagree with them. It has become more and more sectarian. This means different groups of people in the government fight with one another and try to grab power only for themselves. Thus, many people believe that the government that came to power after Saddam Hussein will fall too . . . just as he did.[1]

Why do they believe this?

Part of the reason is that, in addition to daily violence, many parts of Iraq do not have electricity and they don't have clean water to drink. Even worse, they don't have health care. There are few jobs available. Because of that, some young men turn to crime, or they join groups of men who want to destroy the current government. Even though there are not as many bombings and killings as there were when the new Iraqi government took power in 2006, there are still too many.[2] "In some parts of the country, violence has reached urgent proportions, with nearly 1,000 people killed in October alone, according to the United Nations."[3]

In some parts of Iraq, there are daily protests against the government, against corruption, and against violence. Sheikh Khaled Hamoud Al-Jumaili, a leader of the demonstrations said,

"We demand an end to checkpoints surrounding Fallujah. We demand they allow in the press. We demand they end their unlawful home raids and detentions. We demand an end to federalism and gangsters and secret prisons!"[4]

Because many of these demands go unheard, there are people who demand a change in the government itself. "We will not stop these demonstrations. This one we have labeled 'last chance Friday' because it is the government's last chance to listen to us," said Sheikh Al-Jumaili. The only thing people like the Sheikh feel is certain, is that there will be more chaos, more violence, and more uncertainty.

Things like no clean water, no electricity, and violence on a daily basis are certainly tough issues for any government to deal with. Iraq's government must also deal with grudges between different religious groups as well as grudges between different tribes and minorities. "All sides hold the others responsible for all the friends and family killed during the Saddam era and the civil war that followed the US Invasion," he said. The government believes that no one can be a true partner for peace, and that each person that smiles may be hiding betrayal.

The government may be right. The terrorist group al Qaeda has increased attacks across the country, and they do so in the name of Islam. This group fights in Iraq with the goal of creating a **caliphate**, which is an Islamic country led by a supreme religious and political leader called a "**caliph**." This is an extremist

---

IN CASE YOU WERE WONDERING

In what ways is it dangerous for kids in Iraq?
According to the UN, terrorist groups like al-Qaida use kids as spies, scouts, and to transport weapons, supplies, and equipment. Even worse, they are sometimes used as suicide bombers.

group associated with a branch of Islam known as the **Sunnis**. Since the United States army left Iraq, al Qaeda has mainly attacked the smaller Islamic branch known as the **Shiites**. They hope to create conflict between the government and the Shiite Muslims throughout Iraq.[5]

Al-Qaeda and many other terror groups that express a belief in Islam are extremists in their views. In other words, they take certain elements of their religion to the extreme. For example, they believe that "faith" is not a choice. They believe if someone does not believe the same way they do, the unbeliever must be forced to believe. This is accomplished through deadly force and terror tactics such as bombings and assassinations to achieve goals they believe God wants them to achieve. This type of Islamic extremism today can be traced to a particular school of thought called **Wahhabism** (wuh-HA-bism).[6]

The last Sunni Caliph of Islam from the Ottoman Dynasty, Abdulmecid Khan II

However, most Muslims in the world today are not extremists, and they do not believe this way at all. The Islamic Supreme Council of America says that "Traditional Islam views religion as a pact between man and God and therefore the

23

domain of spirituality. In this belief, there can be no compulsion or force used in religion."[7] In other words, the majority of Muslims do not believe in violence, or in forcing others to believe the same way they do. Fatima said that, "Muslims are ordinary people, just like people from other religious groups."[8]

There are extremists in most religions, as well as in most political systems. For example, there are white supremacists who call themselves Christians, and they belong to a movement called "Christian Identity," but most Christians do not share their beliefs. Indeed, most Christians would say that these white supremacists were not really Christians at all.[9] It is important to remember that the religion is not what causes problems or extremism. As Tony Blair, the former prime minister of Great Britain wrote, ". . . acts of terrorism are perpetrated by people motivated by an abuse of religion. It is a perversion of faith."[10]

Iraq has its share of problems. Islamic extremism is just one more. If these are the issues faced by Iraq today, the question is, what are the answers to these problems? Some feel that the government must be more open. They believe the government must include more people with views different from the majority. They believe the government must share power more equally between the Shia and Sunni Muslims, and between ethnic minorities like the Kurds. They believe the government must take steps to actively promote peace, and to make sure that even very powerful people always keep the law. The government has to work harder, they say, at fighting terrorism. The government must make basic things like electricity and clean water available to everyone.

If it can't do that, many Iraqis believe it won't be long until the country is once again torn, with almost everyone fighting against those who are different from themselves.[11]

PROBLEMS FACED BY IRAQI KIDS

Most kids don't realize that even though Iraqi kids do a lot of the same things they do, like go to school, they also live in constant danger. There are youtube videos of many children who lost their friends, their family members, and their parents to the violence that has torn Iraq apart. One grandfather talked about his grandson who is in the hospital after having lost his whole family except for his younger sister in a bomb attack in Baghdad in October, 2013. "He asks about his mother and his father and says that he wants to go to school. He still has not learned that his parents are gone."[12]

Other problems kids face include poverty and poor health. In Iraq, there are at least 3.5 million poor kids, and many of these have bad health because they don't have enough to eat. The situation for disabled kids is even worse. They don't have access to the educational system healthy kids do. Moreover, many Iraqi kids today are orphans with no one to look after them.[13]

The government of Iraq is doing what it can, but many say their efforts are not enough. The lives of Iraqi kids are full of uncertainty.

Iraqi siblings
suffer from
birth defects.

This is an Iraqi Kurd. He wears traditional clothing for men.

CHAPTER 4
Minorities in Iraq

As with most countries, Iraq includes more than one culture and ethnicity. The majority of Iraqis are Arab Muslims (either Shia or Sunni Muslims), but there are also Kurds, Turkomans, Assyrians, and others.[1] Christians and other religions make up a very small portion of the Iraqi people.

The Kurds are not Arabs. They have their own language and culture. However, most Kurds are Sunni Muslims. Their language is very similar to Persian, the language of Iran. It is interesting to note that the Kurdish language has such strong regional dialects that a Kurd from the north might not understand a Kurd from the south. Likewise, a Kurd from Iraq may not understand a Kurd from Iran, even though they are technically speaking the same language.[2] Their history is one of oppression. During the Iraq-Iran war from 1980–1988, the Kurds supported Iran (where a large number of Kurds live). Saddam Hussein's government took revenge on them, burning Kurdish villages to the ground. The Iraqi government also used chemical weapons against the Kurdish people. The Kurds tried to rebel against the Iraqi government again after Saddam Hussein invaded Kuwait. However, they failed in this rebellion as well. Because of that, over 2 million Kurds escaped to Iran, but 5 million remained behind. When the Americans invaded Iraq, they tried to help create a safe place for the Kurds in the North of Iraq. Today, the Kurds have a small place in the Iraqi government.[3]

The Turkomans are the third largest ethnic group in Iraq. That doesn't mean there are a lot of them, though. Just as their name sounds, they are related to the people of Turkey. Their language is also similar to Turkish. Many of the Turkomans actually moved to Iraq as part of an invading army from the Ottoman Empire during the 1500s. The majority of Turkomans are also Sunni Muslim. There have been many conflicts between the Kurds and the Turkomans over the centuries, and today the two ethnic groups still do not trust one another.[4]

The Assyrian people are actually the indigenous people of Iraq. That means they are descended from the original Mesopotamians. Specifically, the Assyrians are descendants of the Babylonians and the ancient Assyrians. However, there are not many of them in comparison to the other ethnic groups living in Iraq today. Assyrians make up the country's largest group of Christians in Iraq. Over thousands of years, the Assyrians dwindled in numbers until they became a minority in their own homeland. They have had to defend themselves against aggressive neighbors, fighting to maintain independence. In the end, they were unable to keep that independence, but were able to survive "the Arab, Mongol, and Kurdish conquests in the mountains of Hakkari and northern Mesopotamia," according to Austen Henrey Layard, a British Ambassador to the Ottoman Empire during the 19th century.[5]

Most recently, the government of Iraq has established a province in the north of Iraq in the Nineveh plain specifically for the Assyrian Christian community. This is an important development since many Assyrians have been leaving Iraq for Western countries like the United States over the past few

IN CASE YOU WERE WONDERING

Where did the Kurds come from originally?
Scholars believe that the Kurds originated in Iran during the Middle Ages when several tribes came together in Iran and began living together.

A group of Assyrians take part in a christening at the Church of St. Timothe.

years. Having a place of their own in Iraq, their traditional homeland, may cause many to stay and raise families there.[6]

The largest religious minority in Iraq are the Christians. As of 2013, reported numbers of Christians were only 450,000.[7] Christians in Iraq represent one of the oldest Christian communities in the world. The majority of these Christians belong to several churches including The Chaldean Catholic Church, The Assyrian Church of the East, The Roman Catholic Church, and various Protestant denominations. Iraqi Christians adopted Christianity as their main religion during the 1st century CE. However, since 2003, violence against Christians rose. Many Christians were tortured or killed by Islamic extremists. Because of this, large numbers of Iraqi Christians fled the country and moved to Syria, Jordan, and to Western countries.[8]

The oldest professed faith in Iraq is Judaism, followed by **Zoroastrianism**. The southern Kingdom of Judah (in modern day Israel) was conquered by the Babylonians, and the Judeans were taken as captives to the land of Babylon. The Jewish community of Iraq lasted from the time of Babylon until the creation of the State of Israel in 1948. After this, anti-Semitism rose drastically in Iraq and conditions became so bad that more than 100,000 Jews fled.

The Zoroastrians came to Iraq when Babylon was conquered by the Persian Empire. However, Zoroastrianism declined in popularity after the Persians lost power and today there are only an estimated 40 Zoroastrians left in Iraq.

In addition to these, there are very small numbers of people who follow the **Bahai**. There are also tiny numbers of Kakai (a Kurdish faith) and the Shabak (an independent faith that has elements of both Islam and Christianity mixed in).[9]

One must remember that a lot of the anger and mistrust people in the Middle East have for one another actually goes back thousands of years. In this one region of the world, entire empires clashed with one another, made peace, and then clashed again. Their descendants settled in the same areas and everyone's family remembered the bad things done to them by someone else's family. As the years go by, the cycle of violence, peace, and then violence has touched almost everyone in almost every country of the Middle East.

While the people of Iraq face difficult issues, there are good people in every city and village of Iraq who fight to bring peace for themselves and for their neighbors.

CHRISTIANITY IN IRAQ

The Christian community of Iraq is actually one of the oldest Christian communities in the world. In the book, "By the Waters of Babylon," James Wellard speculates that St. Peter (one of the twelve apostles who were the first followers of Jesus) was talking about a Jewish-Christian community in the area of Babylon when he mentioned "The Church of Babylon." The word "church," in this case was not talking about a church building, but rather a community of like-minded believers. In that time, some Jewish communities around the ancient world were becoming followers of Jesus's teachings. In fact, they were the first followers of Jesus, but soon afterwards non-Jews started following Jesus's teachings as well, and the community in Iraq (which included Jews and non-Jews) was one of the first and largest. Today, most Christians in Iraq are Assyrians, although there are Christians of other ethnicities in Iraq too. The oldest actual church building, according to archaeology, is on the Iraqi-Syrian border. During the 6th century CE, many monasteries were built in Iraq. One of those monasteries became famous as a library, and the Muslim rulers of Iraq in those years relied on the Christian monks to "translate Greek philosophical, medical, and scientific texts into Arabic."[10] That very same monastery still stands today, high on a rocky mountain, but no one knows how many monks still live there.

Iraqi Christians lighting candles for Easter Mass at the St. Joseph Chaldean Church in Baghdad.

An Iraq family having a picnic lunch.

CHAPTER 5
Family Life

Despite its recent war torn history, nothing is more important than family in Iraq. Loyalty to one's family is more important than friends. Family is more important than work. Family is everything! Most families are very large. "I have one brother and three sisters," Fatima said. "We are seven all together."[1] Fatima's family is actually pretty small in comparison to some. That is because it is common for families to keep building on to their homes, and cousins and their families, aunts, and uncles may all live in one big complex. If they don't all live in the same house, many still live on the same street or in the same neighborhood at the very least.[2]

When everyone lives together, guess what happens? Everyone eats together! In Iraq, many family traditions revolve around food. In fact, did you know that Iraq has an official, national food? It does, and it's called **Masgouf**. The name means "impaled fish." Basically, it's a fish on a stick! Iraq also has a national cookie named **Klaicha**. People eat these foods, of course, but there are a lot of foods that seem common to Iraqis that might seem a bit strange and spicy to you. How often have you eaten goat? Unlike in America where hamburgers and fried chicken are common, in Iraq the most common meats cooked for dinner are sheep and goats. However, cows, chickens, and fish are also eaten. Pigs, on the other hand,

Klaicha

Masgouf is a traditional Mesopotamian dish of seasoned, grilled carp. It is marinated in a mixture of olive oil, rock salt, tamarind and ground turmeric. Because it is a fatty fish, it can take between one and three hours depending on the size of the fish, until most of the fat is cooked out.

are not eaten by almost anyone because pork is strictly forbidden in the Muslim religion. Many meals there are cut into pieces, then cooked with onions and garlic, or chopped into tiny bits for stew and then served with rice.[3,4]

If you ever have an Iraqi family invite you for dinner, you should accept the invitation. Not only will you be pleasantly

IN CASE YOU WERE WONDERING

If Iraqi mealtimes are formal, is it considered rude to eat without using utensils?

No. Actually, you can eat with your hands, and you can eat as fast as you want. This can show the host that you love their food!

surprised by the great tasting food, but in Iraq, it is considered a great honor to be invited over for a meal. Guests are always treated with kindness and respect. This is because hospitality is very important to Middle Eastern cultures, and especially in Arabic and Islamic cultures. In fact, there is an Islamic tradition that guests are allowed to stay with a family for up to three whole days before the host can ask how long the guest plans to stay over!

During dinner, some people remove their shoes, and it is polite to ask whether you should too. Some families sit on the floor when eating, with the meal placed on a mat. It is considered very rude to allow one's feet (or shoes) to touch the food mat. Dinner can be rather formal, so being on one's best behavior is important. If you watch people eat, you might be surprised to see that no one eats with their left hand, even if they are left handed! Everyone eats and drinks with their right hand. This is because they consider the left hand to be dirty, and eating with a dirty hand is, of course, rude! You may also have been taught to clean your plate and eat everything you're given, but in Iraq, it is polite to leave a few bites.

Because family is so important in Iraq, you can imagine that marriage is also very important. Marriage customs are different from other parts of the world, especially in the Western World. For instance, many Iraqis marry their first or second cousins. This is because they believe that it is safer to marry a

An Iraqi bride and her new husband cut the cake. Wedding guests celebrate along with the newlyweds.

cousin than someone they've never known. Thus, in Iraq almost half of all marriages are between cousins.

Before the marriage, the bride-to-be usually has a party. At that party, only women are allowed. The women will all tattoo their hands with henna. The women believe the **henna** will bring good luck to the up-coming marriage. Then the day of the wedding arrives. The bride usually wears a beautiful white dress. The wedding ceremony itself is usually held in a special room that has been decorated with flowers. Either on the floor or on a table called the "**Mez al Sayed**," or "Bride's table," is a spread of items that together symbolize good fortune for the future. In more modern weddings, after the ceremony takes place, there is much joyful music and dancing. One of those dances is a new, modern invention that has become popular in recent years. It's called "The Knife Dance." In this dance, a person will start dancing with the cake knife. The bride and groom will offer this person money to get the knife so they can cut the cake. However, the dancing person will usually take the money, and then give the knife to someone else! So the dance goes until everyone is dancing, and only at the end will the last person give the bride and groom the knife. Then the cake is cut, and the bride and groom feed each other the cake!

In the end, the couple leaves to go on their honeymoon. The couple might go to a local expensive hotel or travel to a popular destination. After a couple gets married, the new bride and groom don't usually move in to their own home. Instead, they move in with the groom's parents![5,6]

HENNA WEDDING TRADITIONS

Did you know that the tradition of putting henna tattoos on a woman's hands and feet in complex patterns and swirls is very ancient? In fact, it goes back farther than Islam, Christianity or Judaism. It goes back to the ancient world that existed in the Mediterranean, to its peoples and religions. As time passed, the tradition was handed down from woman to woman, and it stayed even when some of these women married into other cultures and into other faiths. Today, Muslim, Christian, Jewish, and Hindu women throughout the Middle East, India, parts of Africa and many other lands (even some in the United States!) practice this tradition.

Henna is not only for decoration. Some women put on a henna tattoo before her wedding because she believes it is good luck to do so. Muslim women will do it because there is a legend that the Prophet Muhammad's favorite flower came from the henna tree. They say that he also used henna to dye his beard.

During the henna ceremony, a woman gets to be with all her female friends and family members. It's one last chance for her to relax and have fun before she becomes a married woman with all the responsibilities of a family.[7,8]

Sattar Saad from Iraq poses with his trophy after he was named the winner of the Arabic television show "The Voice."

CHAPTER 6
Entertainment and Sports

Every country has particular types of entertainment and sports that are more popular than others. Iraq is no exception. As in most other countries, radio, television, and movies have all become incredibly popular in Iraq. However, while these types of entertainment had a strong beginning, when Saddam Hussein came to power, lots of things changed. For example, satellite dishes were illegal, there was only one news channel, and movies were almost always about praising Saddam Hussein's government. Since the American invasion of Iraq, the movie industry there largely shut down, although some filmmakers are trying to keep it alive. Thus, Iraqis have turned to other forms of entertainment. Music is still widely enjoyed, and there are concerts that many can go to.

Iraqi music has deep roots in the past. Ancient melodies weave their way through even modern pop songs. The oldest guitar in the world was invented in Iraq, and so was the lute, called an "oud," a pear-shaped stringed instrument. There are many popular singers including Shada Hassoun and Ahmad Al Sayad. Today, Iraq's music is evolving. From the time of Saddam Hussein to the present, the lyrics and style of Iraqi popular music has rapidly changed. From the calm, relaxing ballads filled with romantic lyrics to aggressive, modern songs that talk about the realities Iraqis face in day-to-day life, each song is an important part of Iraq's culture.[1,2]

Iraq is well-known for being the home of one of the greatest Arab poets to have ever lived! His name was Abu Al Tayeb Al Mutanbi, and he lived during the Abbasid period in the year CE

915. That's over a thousand years ago! As for sculptures, paintings, and photography, Iraqi artists are only now finding the freedom they need to express themselves creatively. Under the rule of Saddam Hussein, artists of all kinds had to make art that glorified him or his government, and all the art had to be done in very particular styles. Now, however, artists like Hashim Taeeh and his partner Yassen Wami experiment with making sculptures out of cardboard. That might sound a bit strange, but they started using whatever cheap materials they could find when normal materials were very expensive because of the war.[3]

Furat al Jamil, a filmmaker from Baghdad, discussed her process of creating art. She said that "An artist lives in his or her own world. You create your own environment and keep the outside world at bay. I live in Baghdad in a house with a garden and big walls: I can somehow separate the outside world with what's happening inside."[4]

If you are curious about Iraqi art, you don't actually have to travel to Iraq to see it. There are whole galleries full of Iraqi art in Washington, DC, and they can be found at the Smithsonian's Samarra Gallery. There, you can find over 1,000 pieces of art that range from thousands of years ago up until the present day.

Music and art can bring even enemies together for a time. Sports can also bring people together in support of a common cause or goal. In Iraq, soccer games bring together almost everyone in support of the national team. Fatima even noted that soccer is her favorite hobby, and she plays it in her spare time.[5]

IN CASE YOU WERE WONDERING

Is dancing popular in Iraq?
Yes. At least, some types of dancing are popular. One type is a little like belly dancing, and it is called the Hacha'a. In this dance, there are more neck and hand motions and less hip movement. For this dance, a woman needs to have long hair so that she can swing her hair to the music.

One very positive thing is that there are Iraqi soccer players from different ethnicities on the national team. In fact, there are Shi'ites, Sunnis and Kurds on the team. Imagine the feeling of pride when a Kurdish player passes the ball to a Sunni, who then scores! In this case, soccer is a wonderful example of Iraqis working together to achieve a common goal. Due to this cooperation, Iraq became soccer champions of Asia in 2007, and the country could not have been more proud! This victory

Iraqi and North Korean soccer players in a game during the 2008 Olympics.

was so important for Iraq that the news drew tens of thousands of Iraqis of every ethnicity out onto the street in a joyous celebration. After the game, the goalkeeper Noor Sabri (who was one of the game's most important players) said, " You know the situation of the difficulties in Iraq. What we can achieve inside the field, it's a modest thing we can give to our people. We have to show them we are sharing with them the celebrations." Abdul-Rahman Abdul-Hassan, a Shi'ite education ministry employee added to Noor Sabri's words. He said, "None of our politicians could bring us under this flag like our national football team did." Shi'ites and Sunnis all celebrated together and for a while, the country was unified.[6,7]

After soccer, basketball is the most popular sport, although there are not nearly as many fans. Ahmad Raad noted that, "It's our second sport. Iraqi people love basketball," he said. "We have for years." Another player said, "I've loved the Chicago Bulls since I was a child. It was one of the few teams we could watch on TV." Professional Iraqi basketball players don't make millions of dollars like NBA players do in America. Instead, they make only about $400 per month! Iraq's best players compete in the Premiere League, where 16 teams across Iraq play together from September to July.[8]

IN CASE YOU WERE WONDERING

Have Iraqi athletes ever competed in the Olympics?
Yes. But, they have only participated in the summer games, and never in the winter games. Iraq has only won one medal, a bronze in weight-lifting during the summer games of 1960 in Rome.

MODERN POETRY IN IRAQ

Much of Iraq's poetry in recent years has spoken of the same things modern musical lyrics address: War, suffering, and loss. Much of it describes life under Saddam Hussein and the hard times his dictatorship caused. But, not all of Iraqi poetry is sad and bitter. There are still poets who talk about simple things, about life and love, about God, about the beauty of women, cities, and animals.

From the greatest Arab poet, Abu at-Tayyib al-Mutanabbi, who wrote "The desert knows me well, the night and the mounted men, the battle and the sword, the paper and the pen," to modern poets like Abboud al Jabiri, who wrote about the life of a simple dove, Iraqi poetry lifts Arabic heritage and culture to a place of national pride.

Iraqi poetry is usually brief. Poets normally choose to write short, very powerful paragraphs instead of very long poems that tell full stories. Throughout the history of Iraq, the kings and rulers found wisdom, entertainment and inspiration in the writings of the land's poets.

Fie'ry Rashness
by Abu at-Tayyib al-Mutanabbi

Fie'ry rashness may as valour be seen
And nervous anger may cowardice mean
Arms are carried by people everywhere
But not all claws are lion's, nor as keen.[9,10]

People take photos in front of the statue of Iraqi poet Al-Mutanabbi on Mutanabbi Street, Baghdad, Iraq. Mutanabbi Street, located near the old quarter of Baghdad, is the historic center of bookselling, a street filled with bookstores and outdoor book stalls. It was named after the 10th century classical Iraqi poet Al-Mutanabbi.

Images of three warriors on the Ishtar Gate, which guarded the inner city of ancient Babylon built by King Nebuchadnezzar II, 604–562 BC.

CHAPTER 7
Famous Places

Although much of its beauty and ancient glory now lie in ruins because of the many wars that have torn the country apart, Iraq is still known for its remarkable architecture and monuments. Chief among these, and one of the ancient Seven Wonders of the World, are Babylon's Hanging Gardens.[1]

Babylon itself was a massive city. The Greek historian Herodotus wrote in 450 BCE that, in addition to its size, "Babylon surpasses in splendor any city in the known world." The Hanging Gardens of Babylon are said to have been built by King Nebuchadnezzar, who ruled the city for forty-three years. He built them, according to some accounts, to cheer up his depressed wife. Archaeologists believe that the gardens were not actually "hanging." In other words, they were not held up in the air by ropes or cables. Instead, they believe a more accurate description would be the "Overhanging Gardens of Babylon." You see, they believe the gardens were built on terraces or balconies, and the beautiful plants hung over the edges, giving the main buildings of the city the look of a wonderful garden.

Another Greek historian named Strabo wrote that the gardens were made of "vaulted terraces raised one above another, and resting upon cube-shaped pillars. These are hollow and filled with earth to allow trees of the largest size to be planted. The pillars, the vaults, and terraces are constructed of baked brick and asphalt." Today, one can find the ruins of the legendary Hanging Gardens by driving about an hour south of Baghdad. It's important to understand though, that some archaeologists think the Hanging Gardens were not actually

Images of the Tower of Babel and the Hanging Gardens of Babylon. Artists must use their imaginations to depict what these ancient wonders looked like since neither of them exist today.

located at the traditional site. Instead, they believe the Hanging Gardens were actually located in the city of Nineveh.[2]

Another very famous place in Iraq is the site of a "stairway to heaven." The great ziggurat of UR, stands alone among abandoned ruins, out in the middle of nowhere, in the Dhi Qar Province of Iraq. What is a ziggurat, you may ask? It's a massive structure built like a step-pyramid in the ancient Mesopotamian valley. The ziggurat in the city of UR was one of the largest. Today, however, only the foundations survive. Yet, even the foundations are impressive. Archaeologists believe that it originally stood over 100 feet tall. Later additions to the ziggurat made it even taller! You see, ziggurats were built for religious reasons, and were important symbols for this region. Two later rulers tried to make the ziggurat a part of their kingdom's symbols. The first was Nabonidus, the last king of the Babylonian Empire. Saddam Hussein also tried to make the ziggurat a symbol, saying that it was a symbol of Iraqi unity and that it "united the state administratively and politically after it had been divided and split."[3,4]

Yet another amazing location that should be on your list if you ever get the chance to visit Iraq one day is the **Great Mosque of Samarra**. Why should you want to see it? Built in CE 851, it was once the largest mosque in the whole world. More than that, its **minaret**, which is a feature all mosques

Built by King Shulgi, the great Ziggurat of UR is one of the greatest monuments of the Sumerian culture.

This monumental mineret is apart of
the Great Mosque of Sammara.

share, is a tower shaped like a giant spiraling cone. The tower has a spiraling ramp on the outside that winds its way up to the top, so people can actually walk on the outside of the tower![5]

Other interesting places are associated with various Iraqi cities. For instance, in Baghdad there is the Iraq Museum. There, you would be able to see exhibits that show off artifacts that came from some of mankind's earliest villages and communities to those of vast empires. Some of the archaeological artifacts contained in the museum are over 10,000 years old. That means they go back to the dawn of history![6]

In the city of Kirkuk, there is an ancient fortress and castle called the Kirkuk Citadel, which is the oldest part of the whole town. It is believed to have been built sometime between 884 BCE and 858 BCE. Another castle in Iraq is the Erbil Citadel. This fortress is even more exciting than the Kirkuk Citadel because it is believed to be the site of the oldest, continuously-inhabited city in the world. That means that people have always lived in the city since it was built thousands of years ago.

As you know by now, Iraq saw the world's first communities, villages, cities, and empires rise, and it also saw their fall. Writing and literature, science and mathematics, monumental art and architecture, as well as many other inventions began in this Middle Eastern nation. By now, you should have a glimpse of what Iraq, the "Land of Two Rivers" and its many different

IN CASE YOU WERE WONDERING

Are there zoos in Iraq?
There used to be a zoo in Iraq. In fact, the Iraqi zoo used to be the biggest zoo in the entire Middle East. However, after the 2003 war, the zoo became badly damaged, and people stole most of the animals.

The new Jalil Khayat Mosque was built in 2007 by the Khayat family. This great building features two minerets, amazing art work, scriptures from the Holy Quran, and magnificent ceiling lamps.

people are like. You've gotten to take a look at its amazing past, and you know what issues face the Iraqi people today. Like many others around the world, you may wonder if the Iraqi people will continue to suffer high levels of violence, or if peace will ever come to "The Land of Two Rivers."

Like the rest of the world, you probably hope that it does.

IN CASE YOU WERE WONDERING

Does Iraq have dangerous animals?
Yes. Many different types of scorpions live in the Iraqi desert, and some can get as big as eight inches long! A deadly type of snake (one of the world's deadliest, in fact) called the saw-scale viper lives in Iraq.

BABYLON

Babylon was one of the most powerful empires ever to arise in the world, and it rose in Iraq. The ruins of Babylon lie not far from present day Baghdad. The results of different armies and different wars have taken their toll on the ancient city's mighty ruins. If you visited those ruins today, you might see bullet

Ancient Babylon as it looked in 1932.

holes in walls, ditches dug so soldiers could hide, barbed wire, and more. For the past eight years, however, the Iraqi government and United Nations (UN) agencies have been trying to restore the ancient ruins. The goal is to turn at least part of the ancient city into a cultural center, a place where people from all over the world can come and safely see the once magnificent city. Some want to even make a theme park based on the ancient empire. Emad Lafta al-Bayati, the mayor of a nearby village said "I want restaurants, gift shops, long parking lots," he said. "God willing," he added, "maybe even a Holiday Inn."

Some want tourism to become a major source of income for the country. They want people to come from all over the world to see Babylon the way people go to see the pyramids in Egypt. But, they also know that Iraq must become safer before any of these dreams can come true.[7]

This is how portions of the re-constructed city of Babylon looked in 2005.

EASY SUMMAG SALAD

This is a recipe for a very tasty salad using the Middle Eastern spice Sumac/Sumaq. In Iraq, it is known as Summag—hence the name Summag salad.

Ingredients

2 large cucumbers
1 large tomato
¼ medium onion
1 tablespoon sumac
salt
olive oil

Directions

1. Slice the cucumbers in half, length-wise. Slice these halves into semi-circles, each no more than 1–2 millimeters thick. Put the cucumbers in the salad bowl.
2. Chop the tomato into bite-sized pieces—not too large and not too small. Add to the cucumber.
3. Slice the onion into long, pieces and add to the tomato and cucumber.
4. Drizzle about 1 tablespoon of olive oil over the salad and add the sumac and salt to taste. Mix well. Enjoy.

IRAQ CRAFT

CUNEIFORM TABLET

The ancient Sumerians invented cuneiform, the world's first writing system. They didn't have pencils and paper like we do. Instead, these river people preserved their ideas by pressing shaped stiff reeds into soft, damp river clay. When the clay dried, the reed marks—and the language they represented—were preserved forever. Many of these durable clay tablets still exist. In fact, anthropologists know more about life in ancient Sumeria than they do about Europe during the Dark Ages.

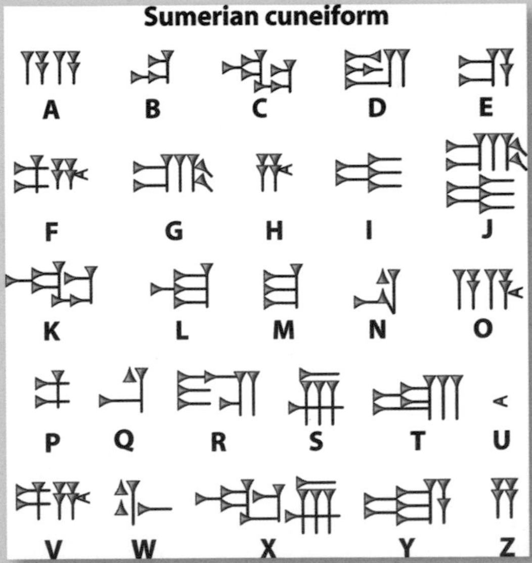

Supplies
2 cups flour
1 cup salt
1 cup water
1½ tablespoons vegetable oil
Mixing bowl
spoon
Wax paper
Rolling pin
Toothpick and a small wedge shape, like the head of a golf tee or a game piece from Trivial Pursuit
Cookie sheet
Butter knife

Sumerian cuneiform

A B C D E
F G H I J
K L M N O
P Q R S T U
V W X Y Z

Instructions

1. Mix the flour and salt together in the mixing bowl. Stir as you slowly add the water and vegetable oil. Mix until you have a smooth, dough-like clay.

2. Turn out the clay onto a very large piece of wax paper. Roll it into a smooth, flat rectangle, about ½ inch thick.

3. Look at the chart above to determine how to spell your name in the cuneiform alphabet. Like English, cuneiform is written from left to right. Write your name out on paper a few times to practice.

4. Write the symbols in your name using proper cuneiform technique! Press the toothpick and wedge or golf tee into the clay to copy the symbols in your name as you wrote them in step 3.

5. Ancient cuneiform scribes would leave their clay tablets in the sun to dry. With the help of **an adult**, you can bake yours in the oven with the same results. Preheat an oven to 250°F. Trim your tablet to a desired size by cutting away extra clay with a butter knife. You can keep the trimmings in a sealed container for another tablet or project. Carry the cuneiform tablet on its wax paper to a cookie sheet. Bake the tablet in a preheated oven for 45 minutes to an hour, or until the project is completely dry and stiff. Set the tablet aside to cool.

WHAT YOU SHOULD KNOW ABOUT IRAQ

Official country name: Iraq

Official language: Arabic and Kurdish. Other languages spoken are Turkmen, Assyrian and Armenian.

Capital: Bagdad

Ethnic Groups: Arab 75–80 percent, Kurdish 15–20 percent, Turkoman, Assyrian, or other 5 percent

Religions: Muslim 99 percent (Shia 60–65 percent, Sunni 32–37 percent), Christian 0.8 percent, Hindu <.1, Buddhist <.1, Jewish <.1, folk religion <.1, unaffiliated .1, other <.1

Area: 169,235 square miles (438,317 square kilometers)

Population: 32,585,692 (July 2014 est.)

Largest cities: Baghdad (capital) 6.036 million; Mosul 1.494 million; Erbil 1.039 million; Basra 942,000; As Sulaymaniyah 867,000; Najaf 779,000 (2011)

Highest point: Cheekha Dar (Kurdish for "Black Tent"); 2.24 miles (3,611 meters)

Lowest point: Persian Gulf 0 mile, 0 meter

Climate: The country is mostly desert, with temperatures mild to cool in winter with dry, hot, cloudless summers; northern mountainous regions along Iranian and Turkish borders experience cold winters with occasionally heavy snows that melt in early spring, sometimes causing extensive flooding in central and southern Iraq

FLAG: Three equal horizontal bands—the top band is red, the middle band is white with green Arabic writing across it that means "God is great. The bottom band is black. The colors are representative of the Arab Liberation flag. The black band represents oppression; the red band represents the country's bloody struggle; and the white band symbolizes a bright future. This flag was approved in 2008 by the Council of Representatives as a temporary replacement for the flag that represented the country during Saddam Hussein's era of ruling the country.

TIMELINE

BCE

5000   The Ubaid (OO-Bayd) culture that became Sumer (Soo-Mer) and Elam (Ee-lahm) rose to power.

3450   The world's first cities appear along the banks of the Tigris and Euphrates rivers.

3200   The world's first ziggurat is built at al-Ubaid.

3100   The writing system known as cuneiform was developed and used for communication.

2700   The Sumerian king, Gilgamesh (Gil-gah-mesh) rose to power. Many epic stories were written about this king, including the Babylonian "Epic of Gilgamesh."

2334   An official from the city of Kish builds a new city called Akkad (Ah-kahd) and crowns himself the new king. He calls himself Sargon 1 (Sargon the First) and he established the world's first standing army. With his army, Sargon establishes the Akkadian Empire.

1900   The Amorites, a Semitic people who lived south of Babylon, swept north and conquered the Sumerians. From that time on, Babylon becomes the cultural and religious capitol of the civilized world.

1800   The old Babylonians invent advanced mathematics based on the numbers six and twelve, and we still use their system for counting hours and minutes today.

1595   The Kassites, an obscure tribe from the Zagros mountains, invade and defeat old Babylon. The rename it "Babylonia"

1157   The Elamit (EE-la-mite) army invades Babylonia and the rule of the Kassites comes to an end.

1114   The Assyrians rise to power, establishing the "Neo" (new) Assyrian period.

859   The Assyrians occupy Babylon and control an empire that stretches from Egypt to Persia.

668   The Assyrian capital, Nineveh becomes the largest city in the world.

609   The Assyrian Empire crumbles and Babylon re-emerges as the world's largest city.

604   The Babylonian king, Nebuchadnezzar (mentioned in the Bible) conquers Jerusalem and destroys the Jewish temple. The Jews are taken captive to Babylon.

540   King Cyrus the Great and his army capture Babylon. The Neo (new) Babylonian Empire collapses and he allows the Jews to return to Jerusalem. The next king makes Aramaic (Air-uh-may-ick) the official language from central Asia to the Mediterranean.

492   All of the Persian armies fall before the advancing Greek army and their general, Alexander the Great.

331   All of Persia and Babylon come under the control of Alexander the Great.

323   Alexander the Great dies in Babylon.

301   Babylon is virtually abandoned after the death of Alexander the Great. A new king rises and builds a new capitol, and a new Empire begins to rise.

CE

116   Persia and Babylon become Roman provinces.

662   Arab armies conquer the Mesopotamian realms under the leadership of Muhammad.

656   The First Islamic civil war occurs.

1258   Baghdad is captured, sacked, and burned by the Mongol leader, Hulagu Khan the grandson of Ghengis Khan.

1536   The Ottoman Empire seizes Bagdad.

1609   The Ottoman Empire loses Baghdad to the Persians.

1831–1914   The Ottomans regain Baghdad and rule it directly.

1920   The Mandate for Iraq and Palestine are awarded to Great Britain by The League of Nations.

1932   Iraq becomes an independent state.

1948   Iraq participates in the Arab League invasion of the State of Israel.

1972   A fifteen year treaty of peace and friendship is signed between Iraq and the Soviet Union.

1980   An eight year war between Iraq and Iran begins.

1981   Israel attacks and destroys Iraq's nuclear research center.

1988   Iraq's government under Saddam Hussein uses chemical weapons against the Kurds.

1990   Saddam Hussein orders the invasion of Kuwait.

1991   The United States and its allies attack Iraq in "Operation Desert Storm." Kuwait is liberated.

2003   Saddam Hussein's government falls and Saddam Hussein is captured.

2006   Saddam Hussein is executed for crimes against the Iraqi people.

2009   A political alliance led by Prime Minister Nouri al-Maliki comes to power.

2014   The United States military presence in Iraq has come to an end. The Iraqi government continues to try and make the country safe for its people. ISIS militants attempt to rule Iraq.

CHAPTER NOTES

Introduction

1. GlobalEdge—Michigan State University, "Iraq: Introduction." http://globaledge.msu.edu/countries/iraq/culture

Chapter 1: A Kid's Life in Iraq

1. Interviews and quotes provided by: Iraqi American Society for Peace and Friendship, 3581 W. Northern Avenue, Suite #8, Phoenix, AZ 85051

2. Arango, Tim. "In Rewriting Its History, Iraq Treads Cautiously." http://www.nytimes.com/2010/06/30/world/middleeast/30iraq.html?_r=0

3. Westall, Sylvia. "After Saddam and war, Iraq's musicians look to home." http://www.reuters.com/article/2012/07/11/us-iraq-music-idUSBRE86A0NV20120711

Chapter 2: History and Government

1. United States Department of Defense—U.S. Central Command , "Timeline of Iraq's History & Culture." http://www.cemml.colostate.edu/cultural/09476/iraq02-01enl.html

2. Ibid.

3. Interviews and quotes provided by: Iraqi American Society for Peace and Friendship, 3581 W. Northern Avenue, Suite #8, Phoenix, AZ 85051

4. GlobalEdge—Michigan State University "Iraq: Introduction." http://globaledge.msu.edu/countries/iraq/culture

5. BBC News Middle East, "Situation of children in Iraq 'a neglected crisis." http://www.bbc.com/news/world-middle-east-22366451

6. Ibid.

7. Ibid.

8. Mark, Joshua J. "Cuneiform." http://www.ancient.eu.com/cuneiform/

9. The Oriental Institute of the University of Chicago, "Ancient Mesopotamia: The Invention of Writing." http://mesopotamia.lib.uchicago.edu/mesopotamialife/article.php?theme=Invention%20of%20Writing

Chapter 3: Current Issues

1. Parker, Ned. "The Iraq We Left Behind: Welcome to the World's Next Failed State." http://www.foreignaffairs.com/articles/137103/ned-parker/the-iraq-we-left-behind

2. Ibid.

3. Pearson, Michael. "In Iraq, a Bushel of Problems Threaten Stability." http://edition.cnn.com/2013/11/01/world/meast/iraq-five-danger-signs/

4. Jamail, Dahr. "Living with No Future: Iraq Ten Years Later." http://www.thenation.com/article/173515/living-no-future-iraq-ten-years-later

5. Laub, Zachary and Masters, Jonathan. "Al Qaeda in Iraq: (A.K.A. Islamic State in Iraq and Greater Syria)" http://www.cfr.org/iraq/al-qaeda-iraq-k-islamic-state-iraq-greater-syria/p14811

6. The Islamic Supreme Council of America, "Islamic Radicalism: Its Wahhabi Roots and Current Representation." http://www.islamicsupremecouncil.org/understanding-islam/anti-extremism/7-islamic-radicalism-its-wahhabi-roots-and-current-representation.html

7. Ibid.

8. Interviews and quotes provided by: Iraqi American Society for Peace and Friendship, 3581 W. Northern Avenue, Suite #8, Phoenix, AZ 85051

9. The Nizkor Project, "Christian Identity: A Religion for Racists." http://www.nizkor.org/hweb/orgs/american/christian-identity/religion-white-racists.html

10. Helm, Toby. "Extremist religion is at root of 21st-century wars, says Tony Blair." http://www.theguardian.com/politics/2014/jan/25/extremist-religion-wars-tony-blair

11. The Center for Strategic and International Studies, "Violence in Iraq in Mid 2013: The Growing Risk of Serious Civil Conflict." http://csis.org/publication/violence-iraq-mid-2013-growing-risk-serious-civil-conflict

12. Al Monitor, "Iraqi children face poverty, violence, exploitation." http://www.al-monitor.com/pulse/originals/2013/11/iraq-children-torn-instability.html#

13. Humanium, "Children of Iraq." http://www.humanium.org/en/iraq/

Chapter 4: Minorities in Iraq

1. Central Intelligence Agency, "World Fact Book: Iraq." https://www.cia.gov/library/publications/the-world-factbook/geos/iz.html

2. Mount Holyoke College, "Kurdish Culture." http://www.mtholyoke.edu/~jlshupe/culture.html

3. The Washington Post, "Who are the Kurds?" http://www.washingtonpost.com/wp-srv/inatl/daily/feb99/kurdprofile.htm

CHAPTER NOTES

4. BBC News, "Who's who in Iraq: Turkmen." http://news.bbc.co.uk/2/hi/middle_east/3770923.stm

5. Layard, Sir Austen H. "Nineveh and Its Remains, Volume 1" (1845), p. 245.

6. BetBasoo, Peter and Kino, Nuri. "Will a Province for Assyrians Stop Their Exodus From Iraq?" http://www.aina.org/releases/20140122133822.htm

7. BBC News, "Christian areas hit by Baghdad bombs." http://www.bbc.com/news/world-middle-east-25514687

8. Damon, Arwa. "Iraq refugees chased from home, struggle to cope." http://edition.cnn.com/2007/WORLD/meast/06/20/damon.iraqrefugees/index.html

9. Vinogradov, A. "Ethnicity, Cultural Discontinuity and Power Brokers in Northern Iraq: The Case of the Shabak," American Ethnologist, pp.207¬–218, American Anthropological Association 1974, p. 208.

10. Young, Penny. "Christians in Iraq." http://www.historytoday.com/penny-young/christians-in%E2%80%88iraq

Chapter 5: Family Life

1. Interviews and quotes provided by: Iraqi American Society for Peace and Friendship, 3581 W. Northern Avenue, Suite #8, Phoenix, AZ 85051

2. Tierney, John. "THE STRUGGLE FOR IRAQ: TRADITIONS; Iraqi Family Ties Complicate American Efforts for Change." http://www.nytimes.com/2003/09/28/world/struggle-for-iraq-traditions-iraqi-family-ties-complicate-american-efforts-for.html?src=pm&pagewanted=1

3. Random Facts, "89 Interesting Facts About Iraq." http://facts.randomhistory.com/interesting-facts-about-iraq.html

4. Food in Every Country, "Foods of the Iraqis." http://www.foodbycountry.com/Germany-to-Japan/Iraq.html

5. Sarhan, Afif. "Iraqi Wedding Traditions." http://www.onislam.net/english/culture-and-entertainment/traditions/409236--iraqi-wedding-traditions-.html

6. aliraqi, "A Traditional Iraqi Wedding." http://www.aliraqi.org/forums/showthread.php?t=99010

7. The Henna Page, "Articles on Bridal Henna." http://www.hennapage.com/henna/encyclopedia/bride/

8. Cvitanic, Dr. Marilyn, Ph.D. "Henna: An Enduring Tradition." http://www.habiba.org/culture.html

Chapter 6 Entertainment and Sports

1. Listen Arabic, "Iraqi Singers." http://www.listenarabic.com/Music+Iraq/

2. Embassy of the Republic of Iraq, "Art and Culture." http://www.iraqiembassy.us/page/art-and-culture

3. Higgins, Charlotte. "Venice Biennale: Iraq's art world emerges from the ruins." http://www.theguardian.com/artanddesign/2013/may/29/venice-biennale-iraq-pavilion

4. Ibid.

5. Interviews and quotes provided by: Iraqi American Society for Peace and Friendship, 3581 W. Northern Avenue, Suite #8, Phoenix, AZ 85051

6. Harden, Nathan. "Soccer Could Save Iraq." http://www.huffingtonpost.com/nathan-harden/soccer-could-save-iraq_b_662003.html

7. Karon, Tony. "Soccer in Iraq." http://content.time.com/time/world/article/0,8599,1647039,00.html

8. Jervis, Rick. "Love of basketball brings players, fans back to court." http://usatoday30.usatoday.com/news/world/iraq/2006-12-28-iraq-week_x.htm

9. Hunter, Poem. "Abu at-Tayyib al-Mutanabbi." http://www.poemhunter.com/poem/fie-ry-rashness/

10. Nick, Martin. "Al Mutanabbi: The Greatest Arabic Poet." http://www.alshindagah.com/sepoct2003/almutanabbi.html

Chapter 7: Famous Places

1. Famous Wonders, "Iraq." http://famouswonders.com/middle-east/iraq/

2. Seven Wonders of the Ancient, "The Hanging Gardens of Babylon." http://www.unmuseum.org/hangg.htm

3. Ancient Worlds, "A Stairway to Heaven: The Ziggurat at Ur." http://www.ancientworlds.net/aw/Article/759360

4. Taylor, Michael. "Letter from Iraq: The Ziggurat Endures." http://archive.archaeology.org/1103/letter/american_soldier_ur_iraq.html

5. BBC News, "Ancient Minaret Damaged in Iraq." http://news.bbc.co.uk/2/hi/middle_east/4401577.stm

6. The Iraq Museum. http://www.theiraqmuseum.com/

7. Gettleman, Jeffrey. "Unesco intends to put the magic back in Babylon." http://www.nytimes.com/2006/04/13/world/africa/13iht-babylon.html?_r=0

FURTHER READING

Al Monitor, "Iraqi children face poverty, violence, exploitation." http://www.al-monitor.com/pulse/originals/2013/11/iraq-children-torn-instability.html#

Al Monitor, "Iraq Pulse." http://www.al-monitor.com/pulse/iw/contents/articles/opinion/2013/09/iraq-songs-influence-war-violence.html#

aliraqi, "A Traditional Iraqi Wedding." http://www.aliraqi.org/forums/showthread.php?t=99010

Ancient Worlds, "A Stairway to Heaven: The Ziggurat at Ur." http://www.ancientworlds.net/aw/Article/759360

Arango, Tim. "In Rewriting Its History, Iraq Treads Cautiously." http://www.nytimes.com/2010/06/30/world/middleeast/30iraq.html?_r=0

BBC News, "Ancient Minaret Damaged in Iraq." http://news.bbc.co.uk/2/hi/middle_east/4401577.stm

BBC News, "Christian areas hit by Baghdad bombs." http://www.bbc.com/news/world-middle-east-25514687

BBC News Middle East, "Situation of children in Iraq 'a neglected crisis." http://www.bbc.com/news/world-middle-east-22366451

BBC News, "Who's who in Iraq: Turkmen." http://news.bbc.co.uk/2/hi/middle_east/3770923.stm

BetBasoo, Peter and Kino, Nuri. "Will a Province for Assyrians Stop Their Exodus From Iraq?" http://www.aina.org/releases/20140122133822.htm

The Center for Strategic and International Studies, "Violence in Iraq in Mid 2013: The Growing Risk of Serious Civil Conflict." http://csis.org/publication/violence-iraq-mid-2013-growing-risk-serious-civil-conflict

Cvitanic, Dr. Marilyn, Ph.D. "Henna: An Enduring Tradition." http://www.habiba.org/culture.html

Damon, Arwa, "Iraq refugees chased from home, struggle to cope." http://edition.cnn.com/2007/WORLD/meast/06/20/damon.iraqrefugees/index.html

Embassy of the Republic of Iraq, "Art and Culture." http://www.iraqiembassy.us/page/art-and-culture

Famous Wonders, "Iraq." http://famouswonders.com/middle-east/iraq/

Food in Every Country, "Foods of the Iraqis." http://www.foodbycountry.com/Germany-to-Japan/Iraq.html

Gettleman, Jeffrey. "Unesco intends to put the magic back in Babylon." http://www.nytimes.com/2006/04/13/world/africa/13iht-babylon.html?_r=0

globalEdge—Michigan State University, "Iraq: Introduction." http://globaledge.msu.edu/countries/iraq/culture

Harden, Nathan. "Soccer Could Save Iraq." http://www.huffingtonpost.com/nathan-harden/soccer-could-save-iraq_b_662003.html

Helm, Toby. "Extremist religion is at root of 21st-century wars, says Tony Blair." http://www.theguardian.com/politics/2014/jan/25/extremist-religion-wars-tony-blair

The Henna Page, "Articles on Bridal Henna." http://www.hennapage.com/henna/encyclopedia/bride/

Higgins, Charlotte. "Venice Biennale: Iraq's art world emerges from the ruins." http://www.theguardian.com/artanddesign/2013/may/29/venice-biennale-iraq-pavilion

Humanium, "Children of Iraq." http://www.humanium.org/en/iraq/

Interviews and quotes provided by: Iraqi American Society for Peace and Friendship, 3581 W. Northern Avenue, Suite #8, Phoenix, AZ 85051

The Iraq Museum. http://www.theiraqmuseum.com/

The Islamic Supreme Council of America, "Islamic Radicalism: Its Wahhabi Roots and Current Representation." http://www.islamicsupremecouncil.org/understanding-islam/anti-extremism/7-islamic-radicalism-its-wahhabi-roots-and-current-representation.html

Jamail, Dahr. "Living with No Future: Iraq Ten Years Later." http://www.thenation.com/article/173515/living-no-future-iraq-ten-years-later

Jervis, Rick. "Love of basketball brings players, fans back to court." http://usatoday30.usatoday.com/news/world/iraq/2006-12-28-iraq-week_x.htm

FURTHER READING

Karon, Tony, "Soccer in Iraq." http://content.time.com/time/world/article/0,8599,1647039,00.html

Laub, Zachary and Masters, Jonathan. "Al Qaeda in Iraq: (A.K.A. Islamic State in Iraq and Greater Syria.)" http://www.cfr.org/iraq/al-qaeda-iraq-k-islamic-state-iraq-greater-syria/p14811

Layard, Sir Austen H. "Nineveh and Its Remains, Volume 1" (1845), p. 245.

Listen Arabic "Iraqi Singers." http://www.listenarabic.com/Music+Iraq/

Mark, Joshua J. "Cuneiform." http://www.ancient.eu.com/cuneiform/

Mount Holyoke College, "Kurdish Culture." http://www.mtholyoke.edu/~jlshupe/culture.html

Nehardea: Journal of the Babylonian Jewry Heritage Center, "Jews of Iraq in Recent Generations." http://www.babylonjewry.org.il/new/english/nehardea/14/10.htm

Nick, Martin. "Al Mutanabbi: The Greatest Arabic Poet." http://www.alshindagah.com/sepoct2003/almutanabbi.html

The Nizkor Project, "Christian Identity: A Religion for Racists." http://www.nizkor.org/hweb/orgs/american/christian-identity/religion-white-racists.html

The Oriental Institute of the University of Chicago, "Ancient Mesopotamia: The Invention of Writing." http://oi.uchicago.edu/OI/MUS/ED/TRC/MESO/writing.html

Parker, Ned. "The Iraq We Left Behind: Welcome to the World's Next Failed State." http://www.foreignaffairs.com/articles/137103/ned-parker/the-iraq-we-left-behind

Pearson, Michael. "In Iraq, a Bushel of Problems Threaten Stability." http://edition.cnn.com/2013/11/01/world/meast/iraq-five-danger-signs/

Poem Hunter, "Abu at-Tayyib al-Mutanabbi." http://www.poemhunter.com/poem/fie-ry-rashness/

Random Facts "89 Interesting Facts About Iraq." http://facts.randomhistory.com/interesting-facts-about-iraq.html

Sarhan, Afif. "Iraqi Wedding Traditions." http://www.onislam.net/english/culture-and-entertainment/traditions/409236--iraqi-wedding-traditions-.html

Seven Wonders of the Ancient, "The Hanging Gardens of Babylon." http://www.unmuseum.org/hangg.htm

Taylor, Michael. "Letter from Iraq: The Ziggurat Endures." http://archive.archaeology.org/1103/letter/american_soldier_ur_iraq.html

Tierney, John. "THE STRUGGLE FOR IRAQ: TRADITIONS; Iraqi Family Ties Complicate American Efforts for Change." http://www.nytimes.com/2003/09/28/world/struggle-for-iraq-traditions-iraqi-family-ties-complicate-american-efforts-for.html?src=pm&pagewanted=1

United States Department of Defense – U.S. Central Command, "Timeline of Iraq's History & Culture." http://www.cemml.colostate.edu/cultural/09476/iraq02-01enl.html

The Washington Post, "Who are the Kurds?" http://www.washingtonpost.com/wp-srv/inatl/daily/feb99/kurdprofile.htm

Vinogradov, A. "Ethnicity, Cultural Discontinuity and Power Brokers in Northern Iraq: The Case of the Shabak", American Ethnologist, pp.207-218, American Anthropological Association 1974, p.208.

Westall, Sylvia. "After Saddam and war, Iraq's musicians look to home." http://www.reuters.com/article/2012/07/11/us-iraq-music-idUSBRE86A0NV20120711

Young, Penny. "Christians in Iraq." http://www.historytoday.com/penny-young/christians-in%E2%80%88iraq

GLOSSARY

Al Qaeda (al Kay-dah)—A global militant Islamist terror group.

Arab (Air-ab)—Arabs are a group of people of different ethnic origins joined together through a common culture, traditions and language. They primarily live in Western Asia, North Africa, and parts of the Horn of Africa.

Armenian (Ar-meen-ee-uhn)—A very small ethnic group in Iraq native to the Armenian Highland.

Assyrians (Ah-sih-ree-uhns)—Assyrians trace their ancestry back to the Sumero-Akkadian civilization that emerged in Mesopotamia. Today they are a minority ethnic group in Iraq.

Bahai (Bah-hi)—A monotheistic religion emphasizing the spiritual unity of all humankind.

caliph (Kahl-leef)—The head of state in a Caliphate.

Caliphate (Kahl-ee-fate)—An Islamic state led by a supreme religious and political leader known as a caliph—i.e. "successor"—to Muhammad and the other prophets of Islam.

Christians (Kris-tee-uns)—Followers of Jesus of Nazareth.

cuneiform (cue-nay-ih-form)—One of the earliest known systems of writing distinguished by its wedge-shaped marks on clay tablets.

Epic of Gilgamesh (Gil-gah-mesh)—An epic poem from Mesopotamia. It is amongs the earliest surviving works of literature.

Great Mosque of Samarra (Mosk of Sah-mar-ah)—A ninth-century mosque located in Samarra, Iraq.

Haram—Forbidden

henna (Hen-uh)—The name henna refers to the dye prepared from the plant and the art of temporary tattooing based on those dyes.

klaicha (Clay-Shah)—Considered the national cookie of Iraq.

Kurds (Kerds)—An ethnic group in Western Asia, mostly inhabiting a region known as Kurdistan, which includes adjacent parts of Iran, Iraq, Syria, and Turkey.

masgouf (Mahs-GOOF)—A traditional Mesopotamian dish, consisting of seasoned, grilled carp. It is also considered the national dish of Iraq.

Mez al Sayed (Mez al Sie-Yed)—Translated as "The Bride's Table."

minaret (Min-ar-et)—Translated as "lighthouse," this is a defining feature of Islamic mosques.

Muslim (Mus-lim)—A follower of Islam.

Ottoman Empire (AH-toe-mahn)—A Turkish state in existence from 1299–1923.

Shi'ites (Shee-ites)—Also known collectively as "the Shi'a." Followers of Shia Islam.

stylus (stie-lus)—A type of writing utensil.

Sumerians (Soo-mare-ians)—People from Sumer.

Sunnis (Soon-ees)—Muslims that follow Sunni Islam, which is the largest branch of Islam.

Turkoman (Turk-oh-man)—A Turkic people located primarily in the Central Asian states of Turkmenistan, Afghanistan, northern Pakistan, northeastern Iran, Syria, Iraq and North Caucasus.

Wahhabism (Wah-Hab-ism)—A religious movement or sect or branch of Sunni Islam.

ziggurat (zigg-er-at)—Massive structures built in the ancient Mesopotamian valley and western Iranian Plateau, having the form of a terraced step-pyramid of successively receding stories or levels.

Zoroastrianism (Zor-oh-as-tree-uh-nism)—An ancient Iranian religion and a religious philosophy.

INDEX

About the Author

Will Blesch is a freelance commercial copywriter, content writer, social media manager, consultant and travel writer with more than 10 years of experience in media and marketing. He works with clients throughout Israel, the USA, and the English speaking world.

IRAQ